HAPPY
HALLOWEEN
Birthday
Marcy Schaaf

Every child dreams of having a birthday that feels truly magical, but for Joe, that dream was his reality—thanks to a little Halloween magic and his dad's playful imagination. Born on October 31st, Joe's special day was unlike any other. With costumes, candy, and pumpkins galore, his dad, Charlie, spun a delightful tale that made Joe believe the whole town was celebrating his birthday. This sweet, true story is about the joy of childhood, the love between a father and son, and the wonderful way a little imagination can turn an ordinary day into something extraordinary. So, put on your favorite costume, grab a handful of candy, and get ready to join Joe on his very special Halloween birthday adventure!

Copywrite @ Marcy Schaaf 2024
Books By Schaaf
Happy Birthday JOE

On Halloween, Joe's birthday arrived,
With spooky costumes, oh, what a vibe!

His dad, Charlie, had a clever plan,
To make Joe feel like a superman!
TRICK TREAT

"Joe," said Dad, with a wink and grin,
"Everyone's dressed up just for you, my kin!"

"They're going door to door, you see,
To celebrate your birthday, just for thee!"

Joe's eyes grew wide, as big as the moon,
"This is my party? Wow, what a boon!"

Kids in costumes, ghosts, and bats,
All for Joe, with Halloween hats!

"Look at those pumpkins, glowing bright,
They're your birthday candles, lighting the night!"

Joe giggled and twirled in his cape,
Feeling like a hero, ready to escape!

"They're saying 'Trick or treat,'
To give you sweets, isn't that neat?"

Joe believed every word, of course,
His dad was his guide, his mighty force!

Off they went, from house to house,
Collecting candy, quiet as a mouse.

Joe's bag filled up, with treats galore,
He thought, "This birthday couldn't be more!"

"Dad," Joe asked with curious cheer,
"Do they do this every year?"

Charlie chuckled, patting Joe's head,
"For you, my boy, the whole town is fed!"

As the night ended, stars above,
Joe felt wrapped in birthday love.

He drifted to sleep, dreaming of treats,
And costumes dancing on spooky streets.

"Next year," Joe thought, "I'll be king,
Of the Halloween birthday bling!"

His dreams were full of pumpkin pies,
And ghosts giving him big surprise highs!

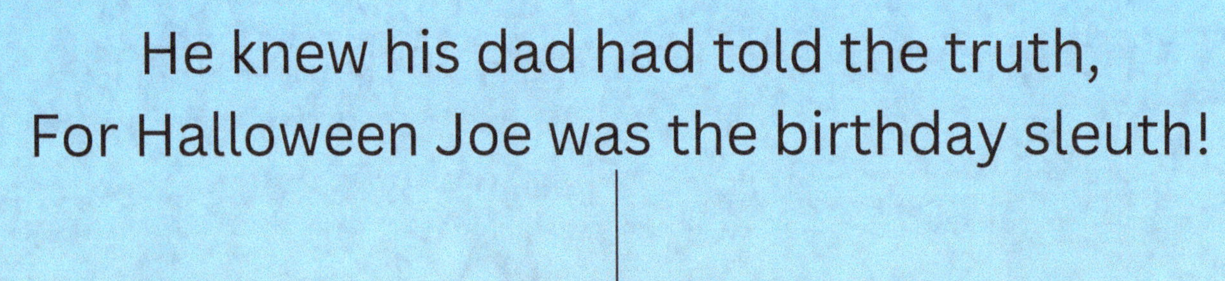

He knew his dad had told the truth,
For Halloween Joe was the birthday sleuth!

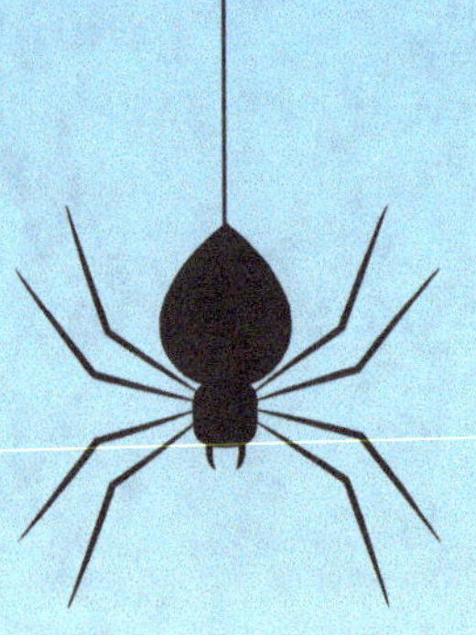

In the morning, Joe woke with a smile,
Thinking, "Next year will be even more
worthwhile!"

But as he grew, Joe learned the trick,
Halloween was for all, not just his pick!

He laughed at the memory, sweet and warm,
Of his dad's funny, birthday charm.

Now every Halloween, Joe would say,
"Thanks, Dad, for making my special day!"

And though he knew the truth by then,
He'd still pretend, every now and then.

That Halloween was his, and his alone,
A birthday fit for a mighty throne!

Joe's birthday fun never did end,
Because every Halloween, he'd play pretend!

So, when you see kids in disguise,
Remember Joe, and his surprise!

For Halloween isn't just tricks and treats,
It's also Joe's birthday beats!

So next Halloween, give Joe a cheer,
He'll be celebrating, far and near!

And in your heart, let the truth unfold,
That Joe's birthday story will always be told!

The End

Books By Schaaf

www.BookBySchaaf.com

find us at:

www.ingramcontent.com/pod-product-compliance
Lightning Source LLC
Chambersburg PA
CBHW082105130726
48003CB00009BA/3060